Conditional
Formatting
Easy Excel Essentials
Volume 2

M.L. HUMPHREY

TITLES BY M.L. HUMPHREY

EASY EXCEL ESSENTIALS
Pivot Tables
Conditional Formatting
Charts
The IF Functions
Formatting
Printing

EXCEL ESSENTIALS
Excel for Beginners
Intermediate Excel
50 Useful Excel Functions
50 More Excel Functions

EXCEL ESSENTIALS QUIZ BOOKS
The Excel for Beginners Quiz Book
The Intermediate Excel Quiz Book
The 50 Useful Excel Functions Quiz Book
The 50 More Excel Functions Quiz Book

DATA PRINCIPLES
Data Principles for Beginners

BUDGETING FOR BEGINNERS
Budgeting for Beginners
Excel for Budgeting

WORD ESSENTIALS
Word for Beginners
Intermediate Word

MAIL MERGE
Mail Merge for Beginners

POWERPOINT ESSENTIALS
PowerPoint for Beginners

.

CONTENTS

INTRODUCTION

In *Excel for Beginners* I covered the basics of working in Excel, including how to format in Excel and how to print. In *Intermediate Excel* I covered a number of intermediate-level topics such as pivot tables, charts, and conditional formatting. And in *50 Useful Excel Functions* I covered fifty of the most useful functions you can use in Excel.

But I realize that some users will just want to know about a specific topic and not buy a guide that covers a variety of other topics that aren't of interest to them.

So this series of guides is meant to address that need. Each guide in the series covers one specific topic such as pivot tables, conditional formatting, or charts.

I'm going to assume in these guides that you have a basic understanding of how to navigate Excel, although each guide does include an Appendix with a brief discussion of basic terminology to make sure that we're on the same page.

The guides are written using Excel 2013, which should be similar enough for most users of Excel to follow, but anyone using a version of Excel prior to Excel 2007 probably won't be able to use them effectively.

Also, keep in mind that the content in these guides is drawn from *Excel for Beginners, Intermediate Excel,* and/or *50 Useful Excel Functions,* so if you think you'll end up buying more than one or two of these guides you're probably better off just buying *Excel for Beginners, Intermediate Excel,* and/or *50 Useful Excel Functions.*

With that said, let's talk Conditional Formatting.

CONDITIONAL FORMATTING

What is conditional formatting and why would you want to use it?

At its most basic, conditional formatting is a set of rules you can apply to your data that help you see when certain criteria have been met.

I, for example, use it in my budget worksheet where I list my bank account values. I have minimum balance requirements on my checking and savings accounts, so both of the cells where I list those values are set up with conditional formatting that will color those cells red if the balance in either account drops below the minimum requirement.

This helps remind me of those requirements, because I'm not always thinking about it when I move money around.

Conditional formatting is also useful when you have a set of data and want to easily flag certain results as good or bad.

You can also combine conditional formatting with filtering so that you first apply your conditional formatting to your data to color the ones you want to focus on and then filter the data using Cell Color or Font Color.

* * *

The easiest way to see how conditional formatting works is to walk through an example.

	A	B	C	D	E	F	G	H	I	J
1	Sale Price	$ 4.99				Conditional Formatting (Red<$1500, Green>$3500)				
2	Payout	70%								
3							Monthly Sales Per Title			
4					15	30	60	150	250	
5				1	$ 52.40	$ 104.79	$ 209.58	$ 523.95	$ 873.25	
6				2	$104.79	$ 209.58	$ 419.16	$1,047.90	$ 1,746.50	
7				3	$157.19	$ 314.37	$ 628.74	$1,571.85	$ 2,619.75	
8				4	$209.58	$ 419.16	$ 838.32	$2,095.80	$ 3,493.00	
9				5	$261.98	$ 523.95	$1,047.90	$2,619.75	$ 4,366.25	
10				6	$314.37	$ 628.74	$1,257.48	$3,143.70	$ 5,239.50	
11				7	$366.77	$ 733.53	$1,467.06	$3,667.65	$ 6,112.75	
12				8	$419.16	$ 838.32	$1,676.64	$4,191.60	$ 6,986.00	
13				9	$471.56	$ 943.11	$1,886.22	$4,715.55	$ 7,859.25	
14				10	$523.95	$1,047.90	$2,095.80	$5,239.50	$ 8,732.50	

(Number of Titles labels rows)

This one is pulled from *Excel for Self-Publishers* and is a two-variable analysis grid that looks at the various combinations of number of titles and monthly units sold per title to project a monthly income number.

(It actually uses four variables because it's set up so you can also change the assumed list price and payout in the top left corner, but the grid itself is comparing the combinations of titles and number sold.)

I've applied conditional formatting to the results to flag in red any cell where the monthly income would be less than $1,500 and to flag in green any cell where the monthly income would be over $3,500.

See how useful that can be? You can easily and visually see where you have to be to meet your target income, which in this case is 150 or more copies sold per month of at least five titles to be "in the green".

To color the cells green, I highlighted the cells I wanted to apply conditional formatting to (in this case E5:I14), then went to the Styles section of the Home tab and clicked on the dropdown arrow next to Conditional Formatting. From there I chose Highlight Cells Rules and Greater Than.

This brought up the Greater Than dialogue box where I entered 3500 in the left-hand field and chose Green Fill with Dark Green Text from the right-hand dropdown.

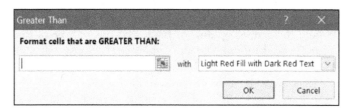

After I clicked OK any cell where the value was greater than $3,500 was colored green with green text.

To color the cells red if the amount was under $1,500 I did the same thing except I chose Less Than under Highlight Cells Rules and entered 1500 in the left-hand field of the Less Than dialogue box and chose Light Red Fill with Dark Red Text.

To sum it up: Highlight your cells, go to the Styles section of the Home tab, click on Conditional Formatting, choose the option you want, set your parameter, and choose your desired formatting.

With the Highlight Cells Rules, you can set parameters using Greater Than, Less Than, Between, Equal To, Text that Contains, A Date Occurring, or Duplicate Values.

I'm not a fan of the Duplicate Values option. First, it doesn't discriminate between different values that have duplicates. So if you have a 7, 8, and 9 repeated twice in a list it will color all of the 7s, 8s, and 9s in the list the same color. Second, it colors all instances of an entry that has a duplicate value. So if you have three 7s, it will format all three of them the same. You have to know this if your goal is to remove two of the three values since you can't just filter by formatting and delete all.

The date option is a bit odd as well because you can't customize it.

It lets you flag a date occurring yesterday, today, tomorrow, in the last seven days, last week, this week, next week, last month, this month, or next month.

Depending on what you want to use it for, those options could be very useful or very limited.

With the highlight cells rules I usually stick with the default formatting options of Light Red Fill with Dark Red Text, Yellow Fill with Dark Yellow Text, Green Fill with Dark Green Text, Light Red Fill, Red Text, or Red Border.

But there is also an option at the bottom of the dropdown menu to apply a custom format. When you click on that option it brings up the Format Text dialogue box. From there you can basically format the cell however you want. For example, I was just able to choose to format my text with a purple font and in italics.

* * *

The next available conditional formatting option is the Top/Bottom Rules. You can format values that fall in the top X of your range, the bottom X of your range, the top X% of your range, the bottom X% of your range, above the average for the range, or below the average for the range.

(While the options are labeled Top 10 Items, Top 10%, etc. when you click on them you'll see that you can adjust the number to whatever you want to use.)

To apply one of these options, select your range, go to Conditional Formatting on the Home tab, click on the dropdown, choose Top/Bottom Rules, and then select the option you want.

If you choose one of the options that includes a number, such as Top 10 Items, a dialogue box will appear with a number value you can change on the left-hand side and the standard formatting options available in a dropdown on the right-hand side.

If you want a number other than 10, so the top 20, the top 30%, etc., change the number.

Formatting works the same as with the Highlight Cells Rules. You can choose one of the pre-formatted options in the dropdown or choose a custom format.

* * *

The next option you have is to add Data Bars to your cells. With data bars, the higher the value, the longer the bar within the cell. It creates a quick visual representation of relative value.

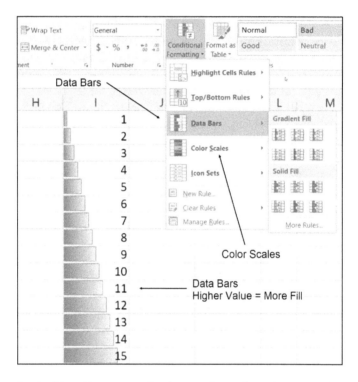

In the Data Bars example above, I have the values in order so you can easily see the bars getting bigger as the numbers increase in size.

To apply data bars to a range of cells, highlight the cells you want to apply the formatting to, go to the Conditional Formatting option in the Home tab, click on the dropdown, choose Data Bars, and then choose from one of the provided color options.

The only difference between the gradient fill options and the solid fill options is in their relative appearance. The example I used above is a gradient fill and you can see how the color fades from darker to lighter across the cell. If you choose solid fill the color will remain consistent across the entire cell.

* * *

Color Scales are another way to show the relative value of cells within a range. With Color Scales the color moves from one color to another as the values in the range increase or decrease.

Aside from the Highlight Cells Rules, Color Scales are the option I use the most.

The default color scale option moves from red for small values to yellow for mid-range values to green for large values, but you can also choose from color ranges that go red-white-green, red-white-blue, yellow-green, or through shades of yellow or green.

You can also choose reverse options of all of the above. So one that applies red to high values, yellow to mid-range values, and green to low values, for example.

I often click on the More Rules options and choose my own colors instead of using one of the pre-set color ranges. However, if you choose to do something like that be careful that the color range you set makes sense.

You don't want to set a color range that moves from blue to green, for example, and then have users not be able to tell which color is "good" and which color is "bad". This is why I tend to use color ranges that move from the light version of a color through the medium version of a color and on to the darker version of a color. Because then it's more intuitive to me which color is the good outcome and which is the bad outcome.

Here's an example of Data Bars and Color Scales with the data in order versus in a random configuration to show how the data might appear in a real-world example where results are in random order:

I	J	K	L	M
Ordered By Size			Random Order	
Data Bars	Color Scales		Data Bars	Color Scales
1	1		1	1
2	2		2	2
3	3		5	5
4	4		9	9
5	5		10	10
6	6		11	11
7	7		12	12
8	8		6	6
9	9		7	7
10	10		8	8
11	11		13	13
12	12		14	14
13	13		3	3
14	14		4	4

* * *

Your last option is Icon Sets which insert a symbol into each cell based on its relative value within the range. You can choose color-coded arrows, circles, or flags. You can also choose a set with x marks, exclamation marks, and check marks. And there are also sets with stars, bars, squares, and circles that are filled to varying degrees depending on the value in the cell.

I'm not a huge fan of the Icon Sets options, but one nice thing you can do with them is turn off displaying the actual values in the cell and just leave the icons to display. You do this under the More Rules option at the very bottom of the Icon Sets dropdown menu.

* * *

By default Excel uses the values in the selected range to determine what a low, mid-range, or high value is.

Because of this I've found that at times I needed to break my data into smaller subsets to have Excel effectively apply conditional formatting to my values.

For example, I was looking at sales by month across all of my titles. When I selected the entire range and applied conditional formatting to it my more recent sales dominated because they were uniformly higher than my earlier sales numbers.

That approach meant that the conditional formatting really didn't tell me much other than I was doing better now than I had been before.

When I went back and only applied conditional formatting to a range of cells for a specific month instead I was able to see which titles each month were my best-performing titles. This allowed me to see trends over time.

(And once I'd done that on one column of values I was able to use the Format Painter to apply that same conditional formatting to each of my remaining columns. I didn't have to select each range and set up the rule over and over again.)

* * *

If you want to set absolute limits instead of allowing Excel to determine your ranges you can do so by highlighting the cells you've applied the conditional formatting to and going to Manage Rules under Conditional Formatting. From there click on the rule you want to edit and choose Edit Rule.

This will let you set the parameters manually.

In the examples below you can see what happens when I edit the default criteria. On the left-hand side are the natural breaks identified by Excel. On the right-hand side are the ones I set. The first example starts at 5, the next has a midpoint set at 4, and the third example sets the cutoffs for each range at 3 for the low end and 8 for the high end.

Excel-Defined Breaks				User-Defined Breaks		
			Start at 5	Midpt at 4	Cutoffs at 3 and 8	
1	1	1		1	1	1
2	2	2		2	2	2
3	3	3		3	3	3
4	4	4		4	4	4
5	5	5		5	5	5
6	6	6		6	6	6
7	7	7		7	7	7
8	8	8		8	8	8
9	9	9		9	9	9
10	10	10		10	10	10
11	11	11		11	11	11
12	12	12		12	12	12
13	13	13		13	13	13
14	14	14		14	14	14

If you choose to set your own parameters be sure to look at your data and confirm that the outcome is what you intended. For example, that one on the right-hand side has a lot of full stars because I set the upper limit to 8 and the values go all the way to 18. Maybe that's what I wanted, maybe it's not.

* * *

To remove conditional formatting from a range of cells or a worksheet go to the Conditional Formatting dropdown, choosing Clear Rules, and then choose either Clear Rules from Selected Cells or Clear Rules from Entire Sheet.

Because of the nature of conditional formatting, be sure that you make the right choice here. Cells can appear to have no conditional formatting on them when they do in fact have conditional formatting in place. So if you're trying to clear all conditional formatting it's best to clear rules from your entire sheet not just from the cells you can see it in.

* * *

It's possible to have multiple rules that apply to the same range of cells. (Like, for example, my two-variable analysis grid above where we had a greater than and a less than rule that applied to the same range of cells.)

In that instance, if you want to remove one of those rules, but not both of them, then go to Manage Rules. This will bring up the Conditional Formatting Rules Manager dialogue box.

Depending on whether you select "This Worksheet" or "Current Selection" from the dropdown at the top of the dialogue box, you will either see all conditional formatting rules that are in place for that worksheet or just the rules that apply to that cell or section.

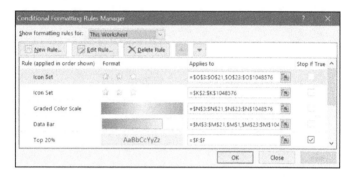

To remove one rule, click on it and then choose Delete Rule.

You can also change the order of the rules when more than one applies to a cell or range of cells and choose to have Excel stop applying rules if one is met by using the Stop if True checkbox.

It's also possible to edit a rule from this dialogue box or to add a new rule from this dialogue box. To edit a rule, click on it and then choose Edit Rule. To add a new rule, click on New Rule.

* * *

You can also add a New Rule from the Conditional Formatting dropdown. This is the new rule option that gives you the most flexibility in terms of setting your parameters. If you click on this option you'll see the New Formatting Rule dialogue box where you can choose any of the types of rules we discussed above as well as a few others.

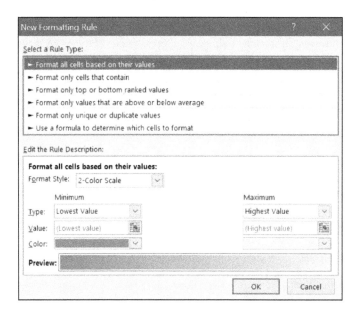

This is probably the best option for creating complex rules with custom parameters, but it's not as user-friendly as the dropdown options are.

(Like with all things in Excel, the options you can access from the dropdowns on the tabs are what you'll need most often, the dialogue boxes are where you go to do everything else.)

* * *

One final point with respect to conditional formatting. At least in Excel 2013 you can combine conditional formatting with filtering. So you can format your cells and then applying filtering and choose to Filter by Color. From there you have the option to Filter by Cell Color or Filter by Font Color. So, for example, if I apply Highlight Cells Rules to a range of cells, I can then filter that data and have it only display for me cells that have green text. Or red text. Or a light red fill color. And you don't even have to know the name of the color you used, because the filtering option will show you the available colors in your data.

This was definitely not an available option in early version of Excel, but it is now and it's very convenient if you can effectively combine the two.

CONCLUSION

So that was conditional formatting. In current versions of Excel I think it's very easy to use, so I do so often. It's a nice way to visually evaluate your results and see what's "good" or "best" in a range of results.

Like I said above, I use it with almost every two-variable analysis grid I build to see where my desired outcomes are going to be. And I use it when looking at my product sales for a month to see which products are selling the best. It's ideal for that type of application.

And, as I just mentioned, you can combine it with filtering to extract results from a large dataset that meet your specified criteria.

The only thing I would caution is to not get too cute with things. In other words, strive for quick comprehension. If someone who doesn't know anything about your data can't look at what you've built and immediately identify "good" from "bad", reconsider your choices. Sometimes checkmarks and exes will make sense to use, sometimes they won't.

Conditional formatting is a very effective tool when used well. But it can add to the noise and confusion when used poorly.

As always, if you have any questions, feel free to reach out and I'll try to help you solve them. I'm happy to help.

APPENDIX A: BASIC TERMINOLOGY

Column

Excel uses columns and rows to display information. Columns run across the top of the worksheet and, unless you've done something funky with your settings, are identified using letters of the alphabet.

Row

Rows run down the side of the worksheet and are numbered starting at 1 and up to a very high number.

Cell

A cell is a combination of a column and row that is identified by the letter of the column it's in and the number of the row it's in. For example, Cell A1 is the cell in the first column and first row of a worksheet.

Click

If I tell you to click on something, that means to use your mouse (or trackpad) to move the arrow on the screen over to a specific location and left-click or right-click on the option. (See the next definition for the difference between left-click and right-click).

If you left-click, this selects the item. If you right-click, this generally creates a dropdown list of options to choose from. If I don't tell you which to do, left- or right-click, then left-click.

Left-click/Right-click

If you look at your mouse or your trackpad, you generally have two flat buttons to press. One is on the left side, one is on the right. If I say left-click that means to press down on the button on the left. If I say right-click that means press down on the button on the right. (If you're used to using Word or Excel you may already do this without even thinking about it. So, if that's the case then think of left-click as what you usually use to select text and right-click as what you use to see a menu of choices.)

Spreadsheet

I'll try to avoid using this term, but if I do use it, I'll mean your entire Excel file. It's a little confusing because it can sometimes also be used to mean a specific worksheet, which is why I'll try to avoid it as much as possible.

Worksheet

This is the term I'll use as much as possible. A worksheet is a combination of rows and columns that you can enter data in. When you open an Excel file, it opens to worksheet one.

Formula Bar

This is the long white bar at the top of the screen with the $f\chi$ symbol next to it.

Tab

I refer to the menu choices at the top of the screen (File, Home, Insert, Page Layout, Formulas, Data, Review, and View) as tabs. Note how they look like folder tabs from an old-time filing system when selected? That's why.

Data

I use data and information interchangeably. Whatever information you put into a worksheet is your data.

Select

If I tell you to "select" cells, that means to highlight them.

Arrow

If I say that you can "arrow" to something that just means to use the arrow keys to navigate from one cell to another.

A1:A25

If I'm going to reference a range of cells, I'll use the shorthand notation that Excel uses in its formulas. So, for example, A1:A25 will mean Cells A1 through A25. If you ever don't understand exactly what I'm referring to, you can type it into a cell in Excel using the = sign and see what cells Excel highlights. So, =A1:A25 should highlight cells A1 through A25 and =A1:B25 should highlight the cells in columns A and B and rows 1 through 25.

With Formulas Visible

Normally Excel doesn't show you the formula in a cell unless you click on that cell and then you only see the formula in the formula bar. But to help you see what I'm referring to, some of the screenshots in this guide will be provided with formulas visible. All this means is that I clicked on Show Formulas on the Formulas tab so that you could see what cells have formulas in them and what those formulas are.

Unless you do the same, your worksheet will not look like that. That's okay. Because you don't need to have your formulas visible unless you're troubleshooting something that isn't working.

Dialogue Box

I will sometimes reference a dialogue box. These are the boxes that occasionally pop up with additional options for you to choose from for that particular task. Usually I include a screen shot so you know what it should look like.

Paste Special – Values

I will sometimes suggest that you paste special-values. What this means is to paste your data using the Values option under Paste Options (the one with 123 on the clipboard). This will paste the values from the cells you copied without also bringing over any of the formulas that created those values.

Dropdown

I will occasionally refer to a dropdown or dropdown menu. This is generally a list of potential choices that you can select from. The existence of the list is indicated by an arrow next to the first available selection. I will occasionally refer to the list of options you see when you click on a dropdown arrow as the dropdown menu.

ABOUT THE AUTHOR

M.L. Humphrey is a former stockbroker with a degree in Economics from Stanford and an MBA from Wharton who has spent close to twenty years as a regulator and consultant in the financial services industry.

You can reach M.L. at mlhumphreywriter@gmail.com or at mlhumphrey.com.

Have you ever wanted to flag results in a data table that matched your criteria? Or wanted to see just by glancing which result in a list of values was the largest value or the smallest value?

That's what conditional formatting will let you do.

Conditional formatting allows you to take a range of cells and highlight those that are above or below a certain value. Or to add icons or bars or colored shading to a cell to show which are your largest or smallest values.

And you can either let Excel determine where to apply those criteria or you can set your own.

Once you learn how to use conditional formatting you will see just how powerful it is for analyzing data.

So don't hesitate.

Learn about conditional formatting today.

ISBN 978-1-950902-31-6
50799

9 781950 902316